School Dropouts: Education Could Play a Stronger Role in Identifying and Disseminating Promising Prevention Strategies

United States Government Accountability Office

Included are the following Collections:

Budget of The United States Government
Presidential Documents
United States Code
Education Reports from ERIC
GAO Reports
History of Bills
House Rules and Manual
Public and Private Laws

Code of Federal Regulations
Congressional Documents
Economic Indicators
Federal Register
Government Manuals
House Journal
Privacy act Issuances
Statutes at Large

United States General Accounting Office

GAO

Report to the Honorable Jim Gibbons, House of Representatives

February 2002

SCHOOL DROPOUTS

Education Could Play a Stronger Role in Identifying and Disseminating Promising Prevention Strategies

GAO

Accountability ★ Integrity ★ Reliability

GAO-02-240

Contents

Tables

Figures

Abbreviations

CCD	Common Core of Data
CPS	Current Population Survey
DPDP	Dropout Prevention Demonstration Program
GAO	General Accounting Office
GED	General Education Development
GRAD	Graduation Really Achieves Dreams
HHS	Health and Human Services
JUMP	Juvenile Mentoring Program
JROTC	Junior Reserve Officers Training Corps
LEA	local education agency
NCES	National Center for Education Statistics
NDPC	National Dropout Prevention Center
PAL	Partnership at Las Vegas
QOP	Quantum Opportunities Program
SDDAP	School Dropout Demonstration Assistance Program
SEA	state education agency

United States General Accounting Office
Washington, DC 20548

February 1, 2002

The Honorable Jim Gibbons
House of Representatives

Dear Mr. Gibbons:

Over the last decade, between 347,000 and 544,000 10th- through 12th-grade students dropped out of school each year without successfully completing a high school program. In October 2000, about 11 percent of 16- through 24-year-olds who were not enrolled in a high school program had neither a high school diploma nor an equivalent credential. These dropouts earn lower incomes, are more frequently unemployed, and have more limited job opportunities than high school graduates. Dropouts are more likely to receive public assistance than high school graduates, and dropouts make up a disproportionate share of the nation's prison and death row inmates, thus imposing a burden on all levels of government. Although the problem has long been recognized, earlier federal efforts to reduce the number of dropouts showed mixed results, and the last significant federal funding for a dropout prevention program ended in 1995. Multiple approaches to dropout prevention exist, and many experts believe that dropout programs should be tailored to the needs of the student population being served. You asked us to examine the dropout prevention efforts currently underway. As agreed with your office, we focused our work on answering the following questions:

- What are the national and regional dropout rate trends?
- What does the research say about factors associated with dropping out?
- What state, local, or private efforts have been implemented to address the factors associated with dropping out?
- What federal efforts exist to reduce dropout rates and what is known about their effectiveness?

In conducting this work, we interviewed officials at the National Center for Education Statistics (NCES) and reviewed NCES annual reports, statistics, and studies related to dropout rates. We also contacted and reviewed the reports of dropout prevention experts at universities, federal agencies, and private research organizations. We conducted site visits at state, local, and private dropout prevention programs in six states—California, Florida, Nevada, Pennsylvania, Texas, and Washington. These programs were selected based on recommendations obtained from a variety of sources, including federal program administrators, evaluations of programs, and program experts. We interviewed, in all 50 states and the District of Columbia, state at-risk coordinators that were either identified by the National Dropout Prevention Center in South Carolina or who were referred to us by state program administrators. In addition, we interviewed officials from the federal programs that could fund local dropout prevention efforts. We also reviewed evaluations of programs funded by the federal School Dropout Demonstration Assistance Program (SDDAP) in fiscal years 1988-1995. Appendix I further describes our scope and methodology. We conducted our review between January and October 2001 in accordance with generally accepted government auditing standards.

Results in Brief

National dropout rates changed little in the 1990-2000 period. NCES—which is the primary federal entity responsible for publishing U.S. dropout data—reports that the national status dropout rate, which is the percent of 16- through 24-year-olds who are not enrolled in school and who have not completed a high school diploma or obtained a high school equivalency certificate, fluctuated between 10.9 and 12.5 percent in the 1990-2000 period.[1] However, dropout rates have varied considerably between regions of the country and ethnic groups. For example, in 2000 dropout rates were higher in the South and West than they were in the Midwest and Northeast regions. In addition, dropout rates are considerably higher for Hispanics than for other ethnic groups, and Hispanics born outside the country are nearly three times as likely to drop out as those born in the United States. Dropout figures also vary depending on which dropout or school completion measure is used, primarily because calculations use different age groups, data, or definitions of dropout. No one dropout measure is ideal for all situations. The status dropout rate is useful in measuring the percent of 16- through 24-year-olds who are not enrolled in school and who have not earned a high school diploma or equivalent credential, but does not indicate how well schools are preventing students from dropping out in a given year. The event dropout rate provides a better measure of how well schools are performing in a given year since it measures the percent of 15- through 24-year-olds who dropped out of grades 10-12 in just the last year.

---

[1]This report focuses on the status dropout rate. According to NCES, this rate reveals the extent of the dropout problem in the population and can be used to estimate the need for further education and training designed to help dropouts participate fully in the economy and life of the nation. This rate includes individuals who may not have attended school in the United States.

Research has shown that multiple factors are associated with dropping out and that dropping out of school is a long-term process of disengagement that occurs over time and begins in the earliest grades. NCES and private research organizations have identified two types of factors—those associated with families and those related to an individual's experience in school—that are related to dropping out. For example, students from low-income, single-parent, and less-educated families often enter school less prepared than children from more affluent, better educated families and subsequently drop out at a much higher rate than other students do. Factors related to an individual's experiences in school often can be identified soon after a child begins school. These factors, such as low grades, absenteeism, disciplinary problems, frequently changing schools, and being retained for one or more grades, are all found at a much higher than average rate in students that drop out. Study of the long-term process of dropping out may provide insights into ways to identify earlier potential dropouts.

A variety of state, local, and private programs are available to assist youth at risk of dropping out of school. These programs range in scope from small-scale supplementary services that target a small group of students, such as mentoring or counseling services, to comprehensive school-wide restructuring efforts that involve changing the entire school to improve educational opportunities for all students. The Coca-Cola Valued Youth Program, for example, supports a tutoring program in which older children tutor younger children, and Project GRAD is a comprehensive school reform model that provides integrated programs for kindergarten through 12th grade students. Several of the dropout prevention programs we reviewed have been rigorously evaluated to determine their effectiveness, and other programs have shown improvements in one or more aspects, such as students' attendance and test scores. States' support of dropout prevention activities varies considerably, with some states providing funds specifically for dropout prevention programs while others fund programs to serve the broader population of at-risk youth, which may help prevent them from dropping out.

One federal program, the Dropout Prevention Demonstration Program (DPDP)—first funded at $5 million in fiscal year 2001—is specifically targeted to dropouts; because the program is new, the Department of Education has not yet evaluated its effectiveness. In September 2001, the program awarded grants to state and local education agencies working to reduce the number of school dropouts. Other federal programs, such as Education's Prevention and Intervention Programs for Children and Youth who are Neglected, Delinquent, or At-Risk of Dropping Out (Title I, part

D), have dropout prevention as one of their multiple objectives, and many more federal programs serve at-risk youth but do not have dropout prevention as a stated program goal. The federal government does not track the amount of federal funding used for dropout prevention services or require that evaluations of programs include assessments of their effect on dropout rates, even for programs for which dropout prevention is an objective. Thus, the total federal funding used for dropout prevention activities or their impact on reducing dropouts is not known. Evaluations of the prior federal program devoted entirely to dropout prevention, the SDDAP funded from 1988 to 1995, showed mixed results, with many of the efforts it funded having little or no significant impact on dropout rates. Experts and state and local officials suggested several ways to improve the effectiveness of federal efforts to reduce the dropout rate, such as creating one source of comprehensive information on promising dropout prevention practices and strategies. We are recommending that Education (1) evaluate the quality of existing dropout prevention research, (2) determine how best to encourage or sponsor the rigorous evaluation of the most promising state and local dropout prevention programs and practices, and (3) determine the most effective means of disseminating the results of these and other available studies to state and local entities interested in reducing dropout rates. In commenting on a draft of this report, Education agreed that dropping out is a serious issue for American schools and that rigorous evaluation of dropout prevention programs is needed. Education said that it would consider commissioning a systematic review of the literature on this topic.

Background

The adverse impact that dropping out of school has on both those who drop out and society itself has long been recognized. Multiple studies have shown that dropouts earn less money and are more frequently unemployed than graduates. Dropouts[2] are about three times as likely as high school completers who do not go on to college to be welfare recipients, and about 30 percent of federal and 40 percent of state prison inmates are high school dropouts[3] thus imposing a considerable cost on all

---

[2]Based on a 1996 study of 25- to 34-year-olds who had dropped out of high school after completing 9 to 11 years of school.

[3]Wirt, John, Thomas Snyder, Jennifer Sable, Susan P. Choy, Yupin Bae, Janis Stennett, Allison Gruner, Marianne Perie, *The Condition of Education 1998*, U.S. Department of Education, National Center for Education Statistics, NCES 98-013, Washington, D.C., (Oct. 1998).

levels of government. Given the multiple adverse consequences associated with dropping out, lowering the dropout rate has long been a goal of educators and legislators.

The 1968 amendments to the Elementary and Secondary Education Act of 1965 established local demonstration projects aimed at reducing the dropout rate. From 1969 through 1976, some 30 projects received $46 million in grants from the Department of Education (then the Office of Education) to develop and demonstrate educational practices that showed promise in reducing the numbers of youth who failed to complete their secondary education.[1] The act was amended again in 1974, when funding for dropout prevention efforts was consolidated with funding for other programs, and states were given the discretion to decide what financial support dropout prevention projects would receive through state-administered consolidated grants. In 1988, the Congress created the SDDAP. The program consisted of competitive grants from Education to 89 school districts and community organizations. In fiscal years 1988-1995, SDDAP grantees received nearly $227 million in federal funds. Authorizations and appropriations for the program ended in fiscal year 1995. The School Dropout Assistance Act was passed in 1994 and authorized funding in fiscal years 1995 to 1999, but was never funded. Dropout prevention program funding was subsequently provided in fiscal year 2001 when Education's Dropout Prevention Demonstration Program received appropriations of $5 million.

Although federal funding for dropout prevention programs has been inconsistent, the National Dropout Prevention Center (NDPC) has existed for 15 years and is privately funded. Many of the program officials with whom we spoke said that NDPC was a resource on which they depended for information. This center is housed at Clemson University in South Carolina and offers various resources to those wishing to implement dropout prevention programs. For example, NDPC manages a database that provides program profiles, including contact information, for model programs located throughout the country. In addition, NDPC provides an overview of the 15 strategies it has identified as being the most effective in preventing dropout. NDPC also contracts with school districts and communities to assess and review the dropout prevention programs in the school district and make recommendations for improvement. Much of this information and additional information on annual national conferences

---

[1]*School Dropouts: Survey of Local Programs*, (GAO/HRD-87-108, July 20, 1987).

and professional development services are available on the center's website: www.dropoutprevention.org.

NCES, part of Education's Office of Educational Research and Improvement, is the primary federal entity for collecting, analyzing, and reporting data on the condition of education in the United States. Since 1989, NCES has annually published data on high school dropout statistics. NCES' most recent publication provides national level data for three measures—event and status dropout rates and high school completion rates.[5] Periodically, NCES also reports on cohort dropout rates.[6] NCES also reports dropout rates for groups with various characteristics (e.g., sex, ethnicity, age, and recency of immigration).

Dropout Rates Changed Little in the 1990-2000 Period and Vary Considerably Between Regions and Ethnic Groups

Nationally, dropout rates changed little in the 1990-2000 period. Rates varied considerably, however, depending on the geographic region and ethnic group.[7] The highest dropout rates occurred in the South and West, while the Midwest and Northeast tended to have lower rates. Dropout rates were much higher for Hispanics than for other ethnic groups, affected primarily by the very high dropout rates for Hispanics born outside the United States. Dropout figures also vary depending on which dropout or school completion measure is used, primarily because calculations use different age groups, data, or definitions of dropout. No one measure is appropriate for all situations. Those using dropout or completion data must familiarize themselves with the various measures and select the one that best meets their needs.

---

[5]Kaufman, Phillip, Martha Naomi Alt, and Christopher D. Chapman, *Dropout Rates in the United States: 2000*, U.S. Department of Education, National Center for Education Statistics, NCES 2002-114,Washington, D.C., (Nov. 2001).

[6]See app. II for a description of each type of dropout and high school completion rate.

[7]The dropout rate referred to in this section of the report is the status dropout rate, which is the proportion of all 16- through 24-year-olds who are not enrolled in a high school program and have not completed high school. This measure is used because it reveals the extent of the dropout problem in the population and can be used to estimate the need for further education and training for dropouts. See app. II for a description of each type of dropout and high school completion rate.

National Dropout Rates Show Little Change in Recent Years

For the nation as a whole, dropout rates changed little in the 1990-2000 period. Data compiled by NCES indicates that the percentage of 16- through 24-year-olds who were dropouts ranged between 10.9 and 12.5 percent. While the year-to-year results went up in some years and down in others, the net result was a decline of 1.2 percentage points during this time period.

Figure 1: Percentage of 16- Through 24-Year-Olds Who Were Dropouts, October 1990 Through October 2000

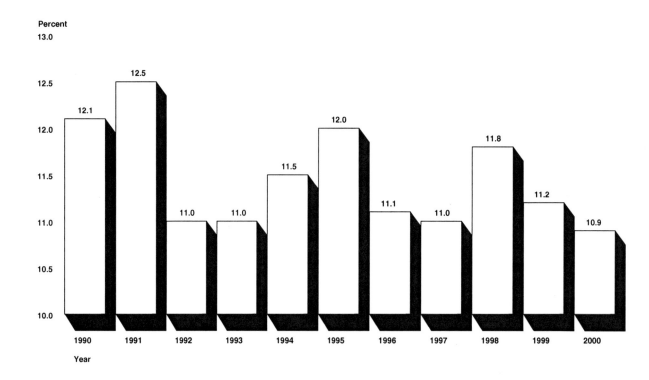

Note: This figure presents NCES' status dropout rate.

Source: NCES, Dropout Rates in the United States: 2000, U.S. Department of Education, Office of Educational Research and Improvement, table C, p. 51.

Dropout Rates Vary Considerably by Region and Ethnic Group

Dropout rates show considerable variation when broken down by region or by ethnic group. The highest dropout rates occurred in the South and West, while the lowest rates occurred in the Northeast and Midwest. As figure 2 shows, while the national portion of 16- through 24-year-olds that were dropouts was 10.9 percent in October 2000, the regional average ranged from 12.9 percent in the South to 8.5 percent in the Northeast.

Figure 2: Percentage of 16- Through 24-Year-Olds Who Were Dropouts by Region, October 2000

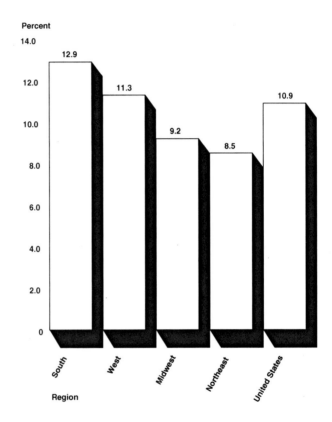

Note: This figure presents NCES' status dropout rate.

Source: NCES, Dropout Rates in the United States: 2000, U.S. Department of Education, Office of Educational Research and Improvement, table 3, p. 13.

Analyzed by ethnic group, dropout rates were higher for Hispanics than for other ethnic groups,[8] as shown in figure 3. For example, in 2000, the Hispanic dropout rate was 27.8 percent compared with 6.9 percent and

---

[8]For an expanded discussion of the nature and extent of the school dropout problems among Hispanics see *Hispanics' Schooling: Risk Factors for Dropping Out and Barriers to Resuming Education* (GAO/PEMD-94-24, July 27, 1994).

13.1 percent for white non-Hispanics and black non-Hispanics, respectively. Asian/Pacific Islanders had the lowest dropout rate, 3.8 percent, in 2000. However, due to the relatively small sample sizes, reliable estimates for Asian/Pacific Islanders could not be calculated before 1998, so they are not shown separately in the trend lines in figure 3. In addition, sample sizes were too small for NCES to calculate dropout rates for American Indians/Alaskan Natives in any year.

Figure 3: Percentage of 16- Through 24-Year-Olds Who Were Dropouts by Ethnic Group, October 1990 Through October 2000

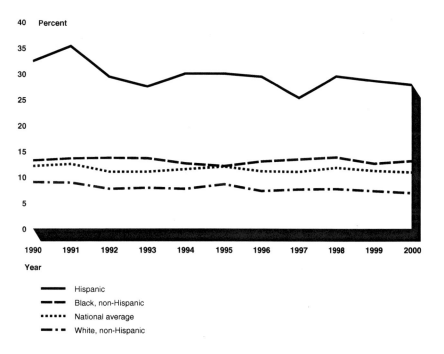

Note: This figure presents NCES' status dropout rate.

Source: NCES, *Dropout Rates in the United States: 2000*, U.S. Department of Education, Office of Educational Research and Improvement, table B5, p. 37.

Further analysis offers additional insight into the high dropout rate for Hispanics. Compared to non-Hispanics in the United States, a much higher percent of Hispanic children were born outside the United States—43.6 percent versus 6.5 percent. The dropout rate for Hispanics born outside the United States was much higher than that for Hispanics born in the

United States in 2000 (44.2 percent vs. 15.2 percent). As a result, although Hispanics born outside the country accounted for only 6.6 percent of all 16- through 24-year-olds, they accounted for more than a quarter of all dropouts in 2000 and thus significantly raised the overall Hispanic dropout rate and the national dropout rate. In addition, data from 1995 show that more than half (62.5 percent) of the foreign-born Hispanic youths who were dropouts had never enrolled in a U.S. school, and 79.8 percent of these young adults who had never enrolled in U.S. schools were reported as either speaking English "not well" or "not at all."[9]

Table 1: Dropout Rates in October 2000 for U.S. and Foreign-Born 16- through 24-Year-Olds

Birth place	Dropout rate (percent)	Percent of all dropouts	Percent of 16- through 24-year-olds
Born outside of the United States			
Hispanic	44.2	26.7	6.6
Non-Hispanic	7.4	3.7	5.5
Born in the United States			
Hispanic	15.2	11.9	8.5
Non-Hispanic	7.9	57.7	79.3

Note: This table presents NCES' status dropout rate.

Source: NCES, *Dropout Rates in the United States: 2000*, U.S. Department of Education, Office of Educational Research and Improvement, table 3, page 13.

The high dropout rates for Hispanics also affect the state differences in high school completion rates. As table 2 shows, the states with the highest rates of high school completion among 18- through 24-year-olds (Alaska, Maine, and North Dakota) have very small percentages of Hispanics, while the states with the lowest rates of high school completion among 18-through 24-year-olds (Arizona, Nevada, and Texas) have very large percentages of Hispanics.[10] Our analysis of the state-by-state information for all 50 states and the District of Columbia shows that two factors—Hispanics as a percent of 18- to 24-year-olds in 1999 and the percentage increase in Hispanics under 18-years-old in the 1990s—account for about

[9]McMillen, Marilyn, *Dropout Rates in the United States: 1995*, U.S. Department of Education, National Center for Education Statistics, NCES 97-473, Washington, D.C., July 1997, tables 16 and 20.

[10]See app. IV for a list of the completion rate for each state and the District of Columbia.

40 percent of the variation in the high school completion rates between states.[11]

Table 2: High School Completion Rate 1998-2000 and Percentage of 18- Through 24-Year-Olds in Selected States in 1999 Who Were Hispanic

State	Percent completion rate for 18- through 24-year-olds, 1998-2000	Hispanics as a percent of all 18- through 24-year-olds in 1999
Maine	94.5	1
North Dakota	94.4	2
Alaska	93.3	5
Arizona	73.5	29
Nevada	77.9	23
Texas	79.4	36
National average	**85.7**	**15**

Source: NCES, *Dropout Rates in the United States: 2000*, U.S. Department of Education, Office of Educational Research and Improvement, table C7, p. 53; GAO's calculations based on Census Bureau data.

Multiple Ways of Measuring School Dropout or Completion Exist, Each Appropriate in Different Situations

Analyzing dropout rates is made more complicated by the fact that multiple ways exist to measure the extent of dropping out—and no one measure is ideal for all situations. For example, one way to measure dropouts is to determine the percentage of students that drop out in a single year. This measure is referred to as an event dropout rate. NCES' event dropout rate measures the number of 15- through 24-year-olds that drop out of grades 10-12 in the past year without completing a high school program. While such a measure can be used to spot dropout trends on a year-to-year basis, it does not provide an overall picture of what portion of young adults are dropouts. If the concern is whether the total population of dropouts is growing, shrinking, or staying about the same, a different measure is needed.

Several ways exist to measure the portion of young adults who are dropouts rather than the percentage who drop out in any given year. In one such approach, referred to as the status dropout rate, NCES measures

---

[11]Our analysis is based on high school completion rates among 18- through 24-year-olds who are no longer enrolled in high school or lower grades, a somewhat different measure than the status dropout rates used earlier in the discussion. We used the high school completion rate because NCES had state-by-state data for all 50 states and the District of Columbia, but did not have status dropout rate data by state.

GAO-02-240 School Dropouts

the percentage of all persons from 16- through 24-years-old who are not enrolled in school and have not earned a high school credential, including those who never attended school in the United States. A similar but somewhat different measure is the high school <u>completion rate</u>. NCES' completion rate measures the percentage of 18- through 24-year-olds who are no longer in school and have a high school diploma or an equivalent credential, including a General Education Development (GED) credential. The status dropout rate and the completion dropout rate differ because they are based on different populations. Only the status dropout rate calculation includes 16- and 17-year-olds and those 18- through 24- year-olds who are still enrolled in a high school program. Because of these differences, the status dropout rate and the high school completion rate are not the simple inverse of each other. Another approach, called the cohort dropout rate, uses repeated measurements of a single group of students to periodically report on their dropout rate over time.

Further complicating the picture, most of the types of dropout measures have at least two rates, which differ because they are based on different age groups, data, or definitions of dropouts. For example, some rates use data for a single year while others use a 3-year average, and some count GED recipients as graduates while others do not. (See app. II for descriptions of each of the published dropout and completion measures we identified.)

Different measures can be used separately or together to examine various dropout trends. For example, figure 4 shows the event dropout rate, the status dropout rate and the high school noncompletion rate. The event dropout rate, which measures only those youth who drop out in a single year, is lower than the other two measures which deal with the percentage of dropout in an age group regardless of when they dropped out. The event dropout rate rose slightly—0.8 percentage point—between 1990 and 2000. However, this change was not statistically significant. The noncompletion rate and the status dropout rate showed similar patterns during the 10-year period, with the noncompletion rate declining 0.9 percentage point and the status rate declining 1.2 percentage points during the period. However, as mentioned earlier, these two rates differ, in part because they are based on different age groups.

Figure 4: Event and Status Dropout Rates and Noncompletion Rates, 1990 Through 2000

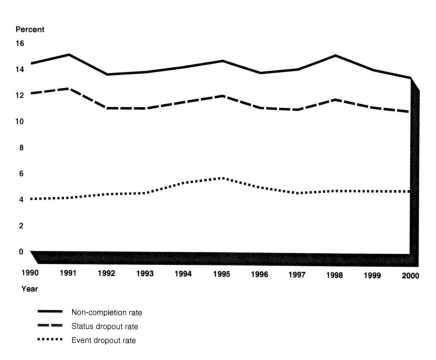

Note: The noncompletion rate is 100 percent minus the completion rate. This rate is used to provide a figure in the same range as the event and status dropout rates.

Source: NCES, *Dropout Rates in the United States: 2000*, U.S. Department of Education's, Office of Educational Research and Improvement, table B1, p. 33; GAO's calculation of high school noncompletion rates.

Another high school completion measure is the "regular" high school completion rate. This rate is the number of public high school seniors who earn a regular diploma in a given year stated as a percent of the number of entering freshman 4 years earlier. For example, in the 1998-1999 school year, public high schools awarded 2,488,605 regular high school diplomas. This number was 67.2 percent of the 3,704,455 students who began the ninth grade 4 years earlier in the fall of 1995. Like all the other dropout measures we identified, the regular graduation rate has its uses, but no one measure is appropriate for all situations. As a result, users of dropout and completion data must familiarize themselves with the many measures available and select the measure or measures which best meet their needs.

Multiple Factors Are Related to Dropping Out

Research has shown that multiple factors are associated with the likelihood of dropping out. Education and private research organizations have identified two main types of factors associated with the likelihood of dropping out—one type involving family characteristics and the other involving students' experiences in school. For example, students from low-income, single-parent, and less-educated families drop out at a much higher rate than other students. Similarly, low grades, absenteeism, disciplinary problems, and retention for one or more grades are also found at much higher-than-average rates among students who drop out. However, identifying students likely to drop out is not just a matter of identifying students with high-risk characteristics, because research shows that dropping out is often the culmination of a long-term process of disengagement that begins in the earliest grades. Study of this long-term pattern may offer ways to better and earlier identify potential dropouts.

Family- and School-Related Factors Are Correlated With Dropping Out

Research indicates that a number of family background factors, such as socioeconomic status, race-ethnicity, single-parent families, siblings' educational attainment, and family mobility are correlated with the likelihood of dropping out. Of these factors, socioeconomic status, most commonly measured by parental income and education, bears the strongest relation to dropping out, according to the results of a number of studies. For example, an NCES longitudinal study of eighth graders found that while data show that blacks, Hispanics, and Native American students were more likely to drop out than white students, this relationship is not statistically significant after controlling for a student's socioeconomic status.[12] Studies have also found that dropping out is more likely to occur among students from single-parent families and students with an older sibling who has already dropped out than among counterparts without these characteristics. Other aspects of a student's home life such as level of parental involvement and support, parent's educational expectations, parent's attitudes about school, and stability of the family environment can also influence a youth's decision to stay in school. For example, results from the NCES study found that students whose parents were not actively involved in the student's school, whose parents infrequently talked to them about school-related matters, or whose parents held low

---

[12]Kaufman, Philip, Denise Bradby, *Characteristics of At-Risk Students in NELS:88*, U.S. Department of Education, National Center for Education Statistics, NCES 92-042, Washington, D.C., 1992.

expectations for their child's future educational attainment were more likely to drop out.

Students' past school performance is also related to the likelihood of dropping out. For example, research shows that students with a history of poor academic achievement, evidenced by low grades and poor test scores, are more likely to drop out than students who have a history of academic success. In addition, students who are overage for their grade or have repeated a grade are more likely to drop out. For example, one study found that students who had repeated a grade as early as kindergarten through fourth grade were almost five times as likely to drop out of school than those who had not. The odds of students who had repeated a later grade—fifth through eighth grade—of dropping out were almost 11 times the odds of those students who had never repeated these grades.[13] Other school experiences related to dropping out include students having a history of behavior problems and having higher rates of chronic truancy and tardiness.

Research also indicates that dropout rates are associated with various characteristics of the schools themselves, such as the size of the school, level of resources, and degree of support for students with academic or behavior problems. For example, a summary[14] of the research on school size and its effect on various aspects of schooling, found that in terms of dropout rates or graduation rates, small schools tended to have lower dropout rates than large schools. Of the 10 research documents that were summarized, 9 revealed differences favoring or greatly favoring small schools, while the other document reported mixed results.

Dropping Out Is a Long-Term Process

Various research studies have focused on dropping out is a long-term process of disengagement that occurs over time and begins in the earliest grades. Early school failure may act as the starting point in a cycle that causes children to question their competence, weakens their attachment to school, and eventually results in their dropping out. For example, a study examining the first- to ninth-grade records for a group of Baltimore school children found that low test scores and poor report cards from as

---

[13]Kaufman, Philip, Denise Bradby, (as above)

[14]Cotton, Kathleen, *School Size, School Climate, and Student Performance*, School Improvement Research Series, Close-Up #20, Northwest Regional Educational Laboratory, 1997.

early as first grade forecast dropout risk with considerable accuracy.[15] This process of disengagement can be identified in measures of students' attitudes as well as in measures of their academic performance. Studies have shown that early behavior problems—shown in absenteeism, skipping class, disruptive behavior, lack of participation in class, and delinquency—can lead to gradual disengagement and eventual dropping out. For example, a report summarizing a longitudinal study of 611 inner-city school children found significant relationships between behavior problems in kindergarten through grade 3 and misconduct in the classroom at ages 14 and 15, future school disciplinary problems, police contacts by age 17, and subsequently higher dropout rates.[16] Study of such long-term patterns that often lead to dropping out may offer ways to better and earlier identify potential dropouts.

A Variety of Programs Address the Dropout Problem

Local entities have implemented a variety of initiatives to address the factors associated with dropping out, ranging from small-scale supplementary services to comprehensive school reorganizations. These initiatives are limited in the degree to which they address family-related factors associated with dropping out, such as income; they focus mainly on student-related factors, such as low grades and absenteeism. While dropout prevention programs can vary widely, they tend to cluster around three main approaches: (1) supplemental services for at-risk students; (2) different forms of alternative education for students who do not do well in regular classrooms; and (3) school-wide restructuring efforts for all students. Several of the programs we reviewed have conducted rigorous evaluations, with others reporting positive outcome data on student progress and student behavior. States' support of dropout prevention activities varies considerably with some states providing funds specifically for dropout prevention programs while others fund programs to serve at-risk youth, which may help prevent them from dropping out.

---

[15]Alexander, Karl, Doris Entwisle and Nader Kabbani, *The Dropout Process in Life Course Perspective: Part I, Profiling Risk Factors at Home and School*, Johns Hopkins University, Baltimore, Maryland, 2000.

[16]Finn, Jeremy D., *Withdrawing From School*, Review of Educational Research, Summer 1989, Volume 59, Number 2, p.131.

Local Entities Use Three Main Approaches for Dropout Prevention

Local entities have implemented a variety of initiatives to address the factors associated with dropping out of school. Our visits to 25 schools in six states—California, Florida, Nevada, Pennsylvania, Texas, and Washington—showed that initiatives in these schools cluster around three main approaches: (1) supplemental services for at-risk students; (2) different forms of alternative education, which are efforts to create different learning environments for students who do not do well in regular classrooms; and (3) school-wide restructuring efforts for all students. Individual programs may focus exclusively on one type of approach, or use a combination of approaches to address many of the student- and school-related factors associated with dropping out of school. Several of the programs we reviewed have conducted rigorous evaluations, and others are reporting positive outcome data on student academic progress and student behavior.

Supplemental Services for At-Risk Students

Providing supplemental services to a targeted group of students who are at risk of dropping out is one approach used by many of the programs we visited. Some of the more common supplemental services include mentoring, tutoring, counseling, and social support services, which operate either during the school day or after school. These services aim to improve students' academic performance, self-image, and sense of belonging. For example, Deepwater Junior High School in Pasadena, Texas, offers the Coca-Cola Valued Youth Program, an internationally recognized cross-age tutoring program designed to increase the self-esteem and school success of at-risk middle and high school students by placing them in positions of responsibility as tutors of younger elementary school students. At Deepwater Junior High, officials told us that about 25 eighth graders tutor kindergartners through second graders at the local elementary school for 45 minutes a day, 4 days a week. Tutors are paid $5 a day for their work, reinforcing the worth of the students' time and efforts. According to officials, the program has improved the tutors' attendance in school, behavior, self-esteem, willingness to help, and sense of belonging. Another benefit of the program is its impact on students' families, such as improved relationships between the tutor and his or her family and between families and the school. The Coca-Cola Valued Youth Program is also the subject of a 1992 rigorous evaluation that compared 63 Valued Youth Program tutors with 70 students in a comparison group.[17]

---

[17]Cardenas,Jose A., Maria Robledo Montecel, Josie D. Supik, Richard J. Harris, *The Coca-Cola Valued Youth Program: Dropout Prevention Strategies for At-Risk Students*, Texas Researcher, Volume 3, Winter 1992.

This evaluation showed that 2 years after the program began, 12 percent of the comparison students had dropped out compared with only 1 percent of the Valued Youth Program students. Average reading grades, as provided by reading teachers of tutors and comparison group students, were significantly higher for the program group, as were scores on a self-esteem measure and on a measure of attitude towards school. The Valued Youth Program has been widely replicated throughout the Southwest and elsewhere.

At another school we visited—Rolling Hills Elementary in Orlando, Florida—officials told us that 85 percent of the students are on free or reduced-price lunches (which are served to lower-income children), and that the school provides multiple supplemental academic programs and social services to address many of the academic, personal, and social problems that are often associated with students likely to drop out of school. These programs and services include pre-school and kindergarten classes to help at-risk children become successful learners, two "dropout prevention" classes for students who are behind their grade level, after school tutoring classes, and a variety of social and counseling services. Progress reports are sent to parents to keep them informed of their child's progress. The school also works with three full-time therapists who help students with their social and emotional problems. Teachers and staff monitor students' attendance and identify early on those with attendance problems. This monitoring effort has resulted in improved student attendance. School officials emphasized the importance of identifying at an early age children who are likely to become academic underachievers, truants, or likely to develop behavioral problems, and the need to develop programs to address the academic and behavior needs of these children. Although longitudinal studies looking at the effects of these services over time would be needed to determine the effectiveness of Rolling Hills' early intervention program at preventing students from dropping out, research suggests that early identification and intervention can help counteract the process of disengagement and withdrawal from school.

Another form of supplemental services provided by schools we visited is school-community partnerships. While a variety of approaches are used by school officials to create school-community partnerships,[18] the

---

[18]For an expanded discussion of school-community partnerships see *At-Risk Youth: School-Community Collaborations Focus on Improving Student Outcomes* (GAO-01-66, Oct.10, 2000).

partnerships we reviewed focused on providing an array of supportive services to students and their families, including mental health counseling, health care, adult education, and recreation programs. For example, the Tukwila School District in Tukwila, Washington, aims to improve student achievement in school by focusing on school, family, and community collaborations. According to officials, the District offers mentoring and tutoring programs, internships, and an array of health and social services. By building partnerships with state and federal agencies, nonprofits, and other organizations, the District hopes to maximize resources in ways that would strengthen young people and their families. A longitudinal study of the District's program during the 1994-1996 school years found that 58 percent of the elementary students who received human services from district service providers and/or community agencies had higher grades than a control group of students who did not receive services, and 74 percent of secondary school students receiving services had improved their course completion rates after two semesters of service.

Alternative Learning Environments

The second approach commonly used by localities we visited is to provide alternative educational environments for students who do not do well in the regular classroom. These alternative learning environments attempt to create a more supportive and personalized learning environment for students to help them overcome some of the risk factors associated with dropping out, such as school disengagement and low attachment to school. Alternative learning environments can either operate within existing schools or as separate, alternative schools at an off site location. Alternative environments operating within regular schools can include small groups of students meeting each day to work on academic skills in a more personal setting, or smaller schools housed within the regular school, such as ninth grade or career academies which focus on a specific group of students or offer a curriculum organized around an industry or occupational theme. Alternative schools located off site are generally smaller schools than those the students otherwise would have attended. These smaller schools usually have smaller classes, have more teachers per student, and offer a more personalized learning environment for students. For example, the Seahawks Academy in Seattle, Washington, is a small alternative school for seventh, eighth, and ninth graders who have been unsuccessful in the traditional middle and high schools. According to officials, the academy is a partnership between Seattle Public Schools, Communities in Schools (CIS),[19] the Seattle Seahawks football team, and

---

[19]CIS is a national nonprofit organization that aims to keep kids in school and prepare them for success in life by bringing health and social services into schools.

corporate partners and strives to provide a safe, nurturing, and supportive learning environment for about 110 students. The school offers smaller class sizes, tutors, mentors, no cost health care, and social services. Students wear Seahawks Academy uniforms and must commit to strict behavior contracts signed by the student and parent. Officials told us that the Academy's policies foster positive expectations and "Seahawks Academy culture," teaching students to respect each other, teachers, and themselves. The Academy emphasizes attendance, academic achievement, and appropriate behavior. Evidence of program effectiveness includes improved test scores, fewer discipline problems, and no suspensions or expulsions for the last 2 school years compared with suspensions of about 7 percent and expulsions of about 0.5 percent at other schools in the district.

Another example of an alternative learning environment is the Partnership at Las Vegas (PAL) Program at the Las Vegas High School in Las Vegas, Nevada. The PAL program is a school operating within the existing school with a school-to-careers curriculum that is designed to provide students with both academic and career-related skills to prepare them for entry into an occupation or enrollment in higher education. Officials said that by linking academic coursework to career-related courses and workplace experience, the PAL program aims to motivate students to stay in school and promote an awareness of career and educational opportunities after high school. According to officials, the program is made up of a team of 6 teachers and about 150 at-risk 11th and 12th grade students. Program participants attend classes 4 days a week and report to a work site for a nonpaid internship 1 day a week. The program features academic courses that stress the connection between school and work and include language arts, mathematics, social studies, science, and computer applications. Essential program aspects include business etiquette lessons, career speakers, field trips, business internships, developing peer and team affiliations, and constant monitoring and evaluation of student progress. According to officials, evidence of program effectiveness includes improved attendance and fewer discipline problems than non-PAL participants. In addition, the PAL program reports a dropout rate of about 2 percent for PAL participants, compared with a rate of 13.5 percent for non-PAL participants.

While only one of the alternative programs we visited has been rigorously evaluated, the others are reporting positive outcomes in areas such as test scores and students' behavior. For example, the Excel program at the Middle School Professional Academy in Orlando, Florida, an alternative school designed to meet the special needs of disruptive, expelled, and disinterested youth, reported substantial gains in mean grade point averages for students in the program. Officials also reported fewer discipline problems and a retention rate of 95 percent for the 2000-2001 school year. The Ranger Corps, at Howard Middle School in Orlando, Florida, a Junior Reserve Officers Training Corps (JROTC) program for about 50 seventh graders, also reported gains of about 15 percentage points in reading test scores as well as increased attendance and fewer disciplinary problems.

School-Wide Restructuring Efforts

The third type of approach used by local entities is school-wide restructuring efforts that focus on changing a school or all schools in the school district in an effort to reduce the dropout rate. School-wide restructuring efforts are generally implemented in schools that have many students who are dropout prone. The general intent of this approach is to move beyond traditional modes of school organization to make schools more interesting and responsive places where students learn more and are able to meet higher standards. Some researchers have suggested that these restructuring efforts have the potential to reduce dropping out in a much larger number of students by simultaneously addressing many of the factors associated with dropping out. An example of a school-wide restructuring effort is Project GRAD (Graduation Really Achieves Dreams) in Houston, Texas—a 12-year-old scholarship program that reports a track record of improving student academic performance and increasing graduation rates. The program was initially established in 1989 as a scholarship program, but in 1993, the program began implementing math, reading, classroom management, and social support curriculum models in a feeder system of schools (all the elementary and middle schools that feed students into a high school). According to officials, the program expanded its services to the elementary grades after program supporters recognized the need to begin intervention in the earliest grades for it to be more successful. Project GRAD emphasizes a solid foundation of skills in reading and math, building self-discipline, providing resources for at-risk children, and offering college scholarship support. Project GRAD has reported demonstrating its effectiveness with higher test scores, higher graduation rates, greater numbers of scholarship recipients, and fewer disciplinary problems in the schools. For example, a 1999-2000 rigorous evaluation of the program showed that Project GRAD students outperformed students in corresponding comparison groups in math and reading achievement tests and made substantial gains in college attendance. The success of Project GRAD has led to its expansion into three additional feeder systems in Houston, with a 5-year plan to expand into two more feeder systems. The model is being replicated in feeder systems in Newark, Los Angeles, Nashville, Columbus, and Atlanta.

Another example of a school-wide restructuring effort is the Talent Development program in Philadelphia, Pennsylvania—a comprehensive high school reform model that aims to improve large high schools that face serious problems with student attendance, discipline, achievement scores, and dropout rates. This model has been implemented in four Philadelphia high schools and approved for implementation in two others. We visited three high schools in Philadelphia that use this approach. According to officials, these schools provide or are in the process of implementing a separate academy for all ninth graders, career academies for 10th through 12th graders, and an alternative after-hours twilight school for students who have serious attendance or discipline problems. Block scheduling, whereby students take only four courses a semester, each 80 to 90 minutes long, and stay together all day as a class, is used in each school. The longer class periods enable teachers to get to know their students better and to provide times for individual assistance. A report on the outcomes of this model at two schools showed that the percentage of students promoted to the tenth grade has increased substantially, and the number of suspensions has dropped dramatically. The report also indicated that students had significant gains on standardized achievement tests in math and improved student attendance.[20]

The career academy model[21] implemented at Talent Development schools and other high schools we visited has been the subject of in-depth evaluations. Career academies represent the high school reform movement that is focused on smaller learning communities. Academy components include rigorous academics with a career focus, a team of teachers, and active business involvement. Extensive evaluations on the academies indicate a positive impact on school performance. For example, in a 10-year, ongoing national evaluation of nine career academies,[22] evaluators compared the performance of 959 students who participated in career academies and 805 similar students who applied to but did not attend an academy. The evaluation also has a long follow-up period,

---

[20]Philadelphia Education Fund. *The Talent Development High School: First-year Results of the Ninth Grade Success Academy in Two Philadelphia Schools*, 1999-2000.

[21]For an expanded discussion of career academies see *At-Risk Youth: School-Community Collaborations Focus on Improving Student Outcomes*, pp. 16-17 (GAO-01-66, Oct. 10, 2000).

[22]Kemple, James J., Jason C. Snipes, *Career Academies: Impact on Students' Engagement and Performance in High School*, New York: Manpower Demonstration Research Corporation, 2000.

which extends 4 years beyond the students' scheduled graduation from high school. One report from the evaluation found that among students at high risk of school failure, career academies significantly cut dropout rates and increased attendance rates, number of credits earned toward graduation, and preparation for postsecondary education. A follow-up report issued in December 2001 stated that although the career academies enhanced the high school experiences of their students, these positive effects did not translate into changes in high school graduation rates or initial transitions to post-secondary education and jobs. [23] For example, some of the students at high risk of school failure obtained a GED instead of graduating. The report also notes that the full story of career academy effectiveness is still unfolding and that longer-term results should be examined prior to making definitive judgments about the effectiveness of the approach.

Most States Provide Programs That Serve At-Risk Youth

Many states have dropout prevention programs or programs that serve at-risk youth that may help prevent them from dropping out of school. Specifically, our calls to 50 states and the District of Columbia found that 14 states have statewide dropout prevention programs,[24] and 29 other states and the District of Columbia have programs to serve at-risk youth that may help prevent them from dropping out of school. Seven states have no statewide programs identified to prevent dropout or serve at-risk youth.[25] Services provided by dropout prevention programs and programs that serve at-risk youth may be similar. However, the number of school districts served and the scope of services offered by either type of program varies greatly by state. Some states provide dropout prevention services in each of the states' districts, while others have dropout prevention programs that serve only a limited number of school districts. For example, Tennessee awards $6,000 dropout prevention grants to only 10 of its 138 school districts annually.

---

[23]Kemple, James J., *Career Academies: Impact on Students' Initial Transitions to Post-Secondary Education and Employment*, New York: Manpower Demonstration Research Corporation, December 2001.

[24]States with statewide dropout programs: California, Florida, Illinois, Indiana, Kentucky, North Carolina, Oklahoma, Oregon, Pennsylvania, Tennessee, Texas, Virginia, Washington, and Wisconsin.

[25]States with no statewide programs for at-risk students: Alaska, Connecticut, Missouri, Nebraska, New Hampshire, New Jersey, and West Virginia.

The following examples illustrate how states implement their dropout prevention and at-risk programs:

- The official dropout prevention programs implemented in California, Texas, and Washington vary in their form and funding. One of California's four dropout prevention programs, the School-Based Pupil Motivation and Maintenance Program, provides $50,000 per school to fund a school dropout prevention specialist (outreach consultant) at 300 schools in about 50 school districts each year. The outreach consultants work to provide early identification of students at risk of failing or dropping out and then coordinate the resources and services of the whole school and surrounding community to identify and meet the needs of these children so they can succeed and stay in school. Texas' dropout prevention program, the State Compensatory Education (SCE) Program, provides state funds to schools that have a large percentage of at-risk students (i.e., students with many of the characteristics associated with dropping out). The SCE program funds services such as supplemental instruction or alternative education with the goal of enabling students not performing at grade level to perform at grade level at the conclusion of the next regular school term. In addition, each district is responsible for developing a strategic plan for dropout prevention. Washington changed its dropout prevention program's focus in 1992 from targeted dropout prevention services to a comprehensive, integrated approach to address many of the factors associated with the long-term process of disengagement from school that often begins in the earliest grades. Washington uses about 15 state programs to help prevent students from dropping out, including programs emphasizing early intervention, schools-within-schools, and community partnerships. How state funds are used to meet state education objectives is largely left up to the school districts.

- Georgia, the District of Columbia, and Utah have no statewide dropout prevention programs, but instead offer comprehensive programs to serve at-risk students. Georgia's comprehensive approach to serving at-risk students provides different services to students of different ages. For example, Georgia has an Early Intervention program for students in kindergarten through third grade, a reading program for students in kindergarten through second grade, and Alternative Education for students who are academically behind and disruptive. State funds are allocated to alternative schools based on a formula grant process. The District of Columbia also takes a comprehensive approach to preventing students from dropping out through a variety of services targeted to at-risk students. Programs include Head Start; after school programs; school counseling; community service; alternative schools that offer small classes, career readiness, testing, and counseling; and a program to apprehend truant students and provide them with counseling and referral services. Federal and District dollars are used to fund these programs. Utah offers a number of programs to serve at-risk students. Programs include alternative middle schools, gang intervention, and homeless/disadvantaged minorities programs. These programs provide mentoring, counseling, and health services to students, and state funds are awarded to school districts through both competitive and formula grants.

Multiple Federal Programs Provide Funds That Can Be Used for Dropout Prevention

The Dropout Prevention Demonstration Program (DPDP)—funded at $5 million for fiscal year 2001—is the only federal program that has dropout prevention as its sole objective; because the program is new, the Department of Education has not yet evaluated its effectiveness.[26] However, other federal programs are also used by local entities to provide dropout prevention services.[27] For example, five federal programs have dropout prevention as one of their multiple objectives and several more programs—such as Safe and Drug-Free Schools and 21st Century Community Learning Centers—serve at-risk youth even though dropout prevention is not the programs' stated goal. Reducing the dropout rate is not a stated program goal of most current programs, and thus assessing how effective the current federal programs have been in reducing the dropout rate is very difficult given that very few programs have been evaluated in terms of their effects on the dropout rate. Prior evaluations of the SDDAP—which have measured program effect on dropout rates—showed mixed results. Although some experts and state and local officials did not believe the creation of additional federal dropout programs was warranted, some of these officials suggested a central source of information on the best dropout prevention practices could be useful to states, school districts, and schools.

[26]On January 8, 2002, President Bush signed into law the No Child Left Behind Act of 2001 (P.L. 107-110). Part H of Title I of the Act is entitled the Dropout Prevention Act, which calls for a coordinated national strategy and creation of a National School Dropout Prevention Initiative to provide for school dropout prevention and reentry and to raise academic achievement levels by providing grants to schools through state and local educational agencies.

[27]For additional discussion of the multiple federal programs that could fund similar services for at-risk youth and for school dropouts see, *At-Risk and Delinquent Youth: Multiple Federal Programs Raise Efficiency Questions* (GAO/HEHS-96-34, Mar. 6, 1996).

One Current Federal Program Has Dropout Prevention as Its Sole Objective, but Multiple Programs Fund Such Efforts

Currently, the only federal program that has dropout prevention as its sole objective is the DPDP. In fiscal year 2001, the Congress appropriated $5 million for the program. The program, in turn, awarded 13 grants of between $180,000 and $492,857 to 12 local education agencies (LEAs) and one state education agency (SEA) with dropout rates of at least 10 percent. These grant recipients are to work in collaboration with institutions of higher education or other public or private organizations to build or expand upon existing strategies that have been proven effective in reducing the number of students who drop out of school. The Stephens County Dropout Prevention Project in Toccoa, Georgia, for example, was awarded $441,156 to screen all 2,400 students in Stephens County in grades 6 to 12 to determine specific needs based on at-risk traits. The project seeks to significantly reduce suspension, grade retention, and repeat offenses leading to expulsion and referrals to the court system through partnerships with the Communities in Schools of Georgia, the National Dropout Prevention Center, and the Department of Juvenile Justice. Another grant recipient, a tribal school located in Nixon, Nevada, was awarded $180,000 to assist approximately 200 Native American students in grades 7 to 12 who have not succeeded in a traditional public school setting to remain or return to high school and graduate by developing individualized education plans.

In addition to DPDP, we identified five programs that have dropout prevention as one of their multiple objectives, with total funding of over $266 million from three federal agencies. In fiscal year 2000, Education received appropriations of $197.5 million to fund three of these programs, and the Department of Justice and the Department of Labor received total appropriations of $69.2 million to fund their programs. Two programs account for most of these funds: Talent Search and School-to-Work. Education's Talent Search program, funded at $100.5 million in fiscal year 2000, provides academic, career, and financial counseling to its participants and encourages them to graduate from high school and continue on to the postsecondary institution of their choice. Education and Labor, who jointly administer the School-to-Work Opportunities Act of 1994, each contributed $55 million in fiscal year 2000.[28] This program's goal is to provide students with knowledge and skills that will allow them to opt for college, additional training, or a well-paying job directly out of high school. Education's Title I, part D program, funded at $42 million in fiscal

---

[28]The authority provided by the School-to-Work Opportunities Act of 1994 terminated on October 1, 2001.

year 2000, provides grants to SEAs for supplementary education services to help youth in correctional and state-run juvenile facilities make successful transitions to school or employment upon release. Two smaller programs that also have dropout prevention as one of their goals are Justice's Juvenile Mentoring Program (JUMP) and Labor's Quantum Opportunities Program (QOP). JUMP was funded at $13.5 million in fiscal year 2000 and aims to reduce juvenile delinquency and gang participation, improve academic performance, and reduce the dropout rate through the use of mentors. Labor allocated $650,000 to QOP in fiscal year 2000 and states that its program goals include encouraging students to get a high school diploma, providing post-secondary education and training, and providing personal development courses.

Twenty-three other federal programs serve at-risk youth, although dropout prevention is not the programs' stated goal. (See app. III for a complete list of these programs.) Safe and Drug Free Schools and 21st Century Community Learning Centers are examples of such programs. Education's Safe and Drug Free Schools Program, funded at $428.6 million in fiscal year 2000, works to prevent violence in and around schools and to strengthen programs that prevent the illegal use of alcohol, tobacco, and drugs. Education's 21st Century Community Learning Centers Program, funded at $453 million in fiscal year 2000, enables schools to stay open longer and provide a safe, drug-free, and supervised environment for homework centers, mentoring programs, drug and violence prevention counseling, and recreational activities.

None of the five programs for which dropout prevention is an objective track the portion of funds used for dropout prevention. However, many state and local officials informed us that they use one or more of these and the other 23 federal programs that serve at-risk youth to address the factors that may lead to students dropping out. The use of programs such as these for dropout prevention is consistent with a recent NDPC recommendation that dropout prevention proponents should look beyond traditional dropout prevention program funding and seek funds from programs in related risk areas, such as teenage pregnancy prevention, juvenile crime prevention, and alcohol and drug abuse prevention to identify and secure grant funding sources.

Few Current Federal Programs' Effects on Dropouts Have Been Evaluated, and Evaluation of Past Federal Dropout Prevention Programs Showed Mixed Results

Since DPDP grants were just awarded in September 2001, Education has not been able to evaluate the program's effect on the dropout rate. In addition, most federal programs that address dropout prevention have other goals, and the measurement of these goals takes precedence over measuring the program's effect on the high school dropout rate. For example, programs that promote post-secondary education as their major goal, such as Talent Search, measure the program's effect in assisting program participants enroll in college rather than what portion of participants complete high school. Also, because many federal programs provide funds for states and localities to administer programs, responsibility for evaluating and measuring the effectiveness of programs is also devolved to the state and local level. For example, Education's Title I Neglected and Delinquent Program mostly administers the distribution and allocation of funds to states. While many of the programs it funds list dropout prevention as one of their intended goals, states are not required to report on their program's effect on dropout rates.

The three major evaluations of the former dropout prevention program—Education's SDDAP which funded demonstrations from 1988-1995—have shown mixed results. A study[29] of 16 targeted programs showed programs that were intensive[30] in nature and that were operating in middle school could improve grade promotion and reduce school dropout rates. However, the same study showed that programs implemented in high school did not affect personal or social outcomes that are often correlated with dropping out (e.g., student's self-esteem, pregnancy, drug use, and arrest rates). The study's authors concluded that dropout prevention programs are more effective when implemented in earlier grades. A second study of SDDAP programs,[31] which focused on the impacts of

---

[29]Dynarski, Mark, Phillip Gleason, Anu Rangarajan, Robert Wood, *Impacts of Dropout Prevention Programs, Final Report*, Mathematica Policy Research, Inc, Princeton, New Jersey, 1998.

[30]Students in high-intensity programs generally remained in the program for the full school day with smaller classes and accelerated curricula designed to help them catch up to their peers.

[31]Dynarski, Mark, Phillip Gleason, Anu Rangarajan, Robert Wood, *Impacts of School Restructuring Initiatives, Final Report*, Mathematica Policy Research, Inc., Princeton, New Jersey, 1998.

school restructuring initiatives,[32] concluded that restructuring would not, in the short term, reduce dropout rates. This study explained that school restructuring was often a lengthy process, and finding the true effect of such efforts on dropout rates could take longer than the 3- to 4-year period of most demonstration programs. This study also explained that although dropout rates were not reduced in schools that restructured, other outcomes such as school climate—the environment of the school and how teachers and students interact— and test scores often improved and that these improved outcomes could ultimately affect the dropout rate. Finally, the third study evaluated 16 programs and found promising strategies for reducing dropout rates at all levels of elementary and secondary education.[33] The study found that at the elementary school level, in-class adult friends (trained volunteers or helpers), after-school tutoring, and enrichment exercises that are directly related to in-class assignments appeared to be effective approaches. At the middle school level, coordinated teaching strategies, flexible scheduling, heterogeneous grouping of students, and counseling services were found to be useful. At the secondary school level, the study found that paid-work incentives monitored by the school and tied to classroom activities were very successful for promoting school engagement. While all three studies of SDDAP programs identified some promising practices or strategies for preventing dropouts or addressing the factors associated with dropping out, none of the programs studied were consistently effective in significantly reducing dropout rates.

State and local officials also had numerous suggestions for reducing the dropout rate. Several of them suggested that Education develop a central source of information on the best dropout prevention strategies. For example, an administrator at Independence High School in San Jose, California, asked that the federal government act as a clearinghouse for information about effective dropout prevention programs, provide a list of people that could be contacted to find out about these programs, and identify programs that could be visited to observe best practices for preventing dropouts. A consultant for the California Department of

---

[32]Restructuring strategies include (1) developing curricular and instructional methods where students have an opportunity to learn more, (2) having teachers play a more active role in managing schools, and (3) encouraging schools to be more sensitive to the concerns of parents and students.

[33]Rossi, Robert J, *Evaluation of Projects Funded by the School Dropout Demonstration Assistance Program, Final Evaluation Report*, American Institutes for Research, Palo Alto, California, 1993.

Education suggested that the federal government could develop model dropout prevention programs and publish information on programs that were successful. The At-Risk Coordinators in Arizona, Idaho, Maine, and New York made similar suggestions for a national clearinghouse or information on best practices for preventing students from dropping out.

As mentioned earlier, NDPC is an organization that provides an NDPC-developed list of effective strategies and information on self-reported model programs on its website. However, the NDPC is completely self-funded through memberships, grants, and contracts and does not have sufficient resources to (1) disseminate information that is available on its database of promising dropout prevention programs and practices, or (2) thoroughly review programs included in its model program listing. Instead NDPC relies on its website to communicate about effective dropout prevention practices and its data are based on voluntary submissions of program descriptions and promising practices by its members and other experts in the dropout prevention field. While some dropout prevention program officials mentioned NDPC as a useful resource, they believe a more complete and current database of program descriptions and promising practices would better serve their needs.

Conclusions

Although there have been many federal, state, and local dropout prevention programs over the last 2 decades, few have been rigorously evaluated. Those federally funded programs that have been evaluated have shown mixed results. Several rigorously evaluated local programs have been shown to reduce dropout rates, raise test scores, and increase college attendance. In addition, some state and local officials believe that they are implementing promising practices that are yielding positive outcomes for students, such as improved attendance and grades and reduced discipline problems, although their programs have not been thoroughly evaluated. Education could play an important role in reviewing and evaluating existing research and in encouraging or sponsoring additional research to rigorously evaluate the effectiveness of state and local programs. Subsequently, Education could disseminate the results of such research and information on the identified best practices for state and local use. Opportunities exist for Education to identify ways to collaborate with existing organizations, such as the NDPC, that are already providing some information on existing programs. As schools continue to look for ways to ensure all students succeed, such research and information could play a vital role in developing and implementing effective programs.

Recommendations

We recommend that the Secretary of Education (1) evaluate the quality of existing dropout prevention research, (2) determine how best to encourage or sponsor the rigorous evaluation of the most promising state and local dropout prevention programs and practices, and (3) determine the most effective means of disseminating the results of these and other available studies to state and local entities interested in reducing dropout rates.

Agency Comments

We provided a draft of this report to the Department of Health and Human Services' (HHS) Administration for Children and Families and the Department of Education. HHS had no comments. Education provided a response, which is included as appendix V of this report, and technical comments, which we incorporated when appropriate. Education agreed that dropping out is a serious issue for American schools, emphasized the importance of school improvement efforts in the No Child Left Behind Act of 2001, and provided additional information about relevant Education programs and activities. In response to our recommendations that Education evaluate the quality of existing dropout prevention research and determine how best to encourage or sponsor rigorous evaluation of the most promising state and local dropout prevention programs and practices, Education agreed that rigorous evidence is needed and said that it will consider commissioning a systematic review of the literature on this topic.

As agreed with your office, unless you publicly announce its contents earlier, we plan no further distribution of this report until 3 days after the date of this letter. At that time we will send copies of this report to the Secretary of Education, appropriate congressional committees, and other interested parties. If you or your staff have any questions or wish to discuss this material further, please call me or Diana Pietrowiak at (202) 512-7215. Key contributors to this report are listed in appendix VI.

Sincerely yours,

Marnie S. Shaul
Director, Education, Workforce,
  and Income Security Issues

Appendix I: Scope and Methodology

To determine dropout rate trends and identify factors associated with dropping out, we obtained and reviewed reports, statistics, and studies developed by the National Center for Education Statistics (NCES), the Annie E. Casey Foundation, and the National Dropout Prevention Center (NDPC). We also obtained the papers presented at the Harvard University Dropouts in America symposium in January 2001 and subsequently made available on the Internet. In addition to interviewing officials at each of the entities listed above, we interviewed dropout prevention experts at universities, federal agencies, and private research organizations and obtained and reviewed their publications.

To obtain information on the services offered by state, local, and private agencies to students who are at-risk of dropping out, we conducted site visits in six states—California, Florida, Nevada, Pennsylvania, Texas, and Washington. We selected these states because our analysis of the literature and discussions with key dropout prevention experts identified a variety of promising dropout prevention programs within these states in each of the major types of dropout prevention approaches—supplemental services for at-risk students, different forms of alternative education, and school-wide restructuring efforts. Between February and August 2001, we also conducted telephone interviews with state at-risk coordinators in all 50 states and the District of Columbia who were either identified by the NDPC or who were referred to us by state program administrators. From the telephone interviews, we determined, among other things, (1) whether the state had a dropout prevention program, (2) if the state had other programs for at-risk youths, and (3) if any evaluations had been made of the effectiveness of the state programs' impact on reducing dropouts. Our review focused only on dropout prevention programs and efforts. We did not obtain information on dropout recovery programs that try to get dropouts to return to school or on programs designed to help dropouts get a General Education Development (GED) credential or other type of high school credential. As a result, our list of programs whose funding could be used to prevent dropouts in appendix III does not include programs aimed only at dropout recovery or helping dropouts to get a GED or other type of high school credential.

To identify what federal efforts exist to address dropout prevention and if they have been proven effective, we interviewed officials from the U.S. Departments of Education, Labor, Justice, and Health and Human Services who manage programs that aid in reducing the dropout rate. We developed our initial list of federal dropout prevention programs through our literature review and updated the list with references made by the various federal program officials. We obtained information on how the programs operated, how funds were dispersed, how dropout prevention was prioritized, and whether or not the programs had been evaluated. We also reviewed evaluations of the federal School Dropout Demonstration Assistance Program (SDDAP), which funded local dropout prevention programs in fiscal years 1988-1995.

Appendix II: Descriptions of Dropout and Completion Measures

Table 3 provides a description of each of the types of dropout and completion measures and the individual measures developed by each of three different organizations. Since 1989, the National Center for Education Statistics (NCES) has annually published a report on dropout rates, *Dropout Rates in the United States.*[1] The most recent report includes status and event dropout rates and high school completion rates. Occasionally,[2] the report includes cohort rates. Both a national and state status dropout rates are developed annually by the Annie E. Casey Foundation for its *Kids Count Data Book.*[3] A second measure of school completion, the "regular" graduation rate, is occasionally published by the Center for the Study of Opportunity in Higher Education in *Postsecondary Education Opportunity.*[4]

Table 3: Dropout and Completion Measures

Measure/source	Description
Event Dropout Rates	**Measures the annual incidence of dropout—that is, the percent of students who leave school in a given year without completing a high school program.**
National Event Rate (NCES)	NCES publishes a national event dropout rate, which it defines as the percent of 15- to 24-year-olds who were enrolled in high school the prior October but had not completed high school and were not enrolled in grades 10 to 12 a year later. According to this definition, a person could complete high school by either earning a high school diploma or receiving an alternative credential such as a GED. The national rate is computed from sample data collected from 50,000 U.S. households by the Census Bureau in its October Supplement to the Current Population Survey (CPS).
State Event Rates (NCES)	NCES publishes state event dropout rates for grades 9 to 12 based on state-reported data collected through its annual survey of state and local public educational agencies, known as the Common Core of Data (CCD). The number of participating states using sufficiently consistent data definitions and collection procedures to be included in NCES' annual report increased from 14 states in the 1991-1992 school year to 37 states and the District of Columbia for the 1997-1998 school year. State data were not available states with large school-age populations – California, Florida, New York, and Texas – in the most recent school year.

[1]Most recently, Kaufman, Phillip, Martha Naomi Alt, Christopher D. Chapman, *Dropout Rates in the United States: 2000*, U.S. Department of Education, National Center for Education Statistics, NCES 2002-114,Washington, D.C., November 2001.

[2]Recently, Kaufman, Phillip, Jin Y. Kwon, Steve Klein, Christopher D. Chapman, *Dropout Rates in the United States: 1998*, U.S. Department of Education, National Center for Education Statistics, NCES 2000-022,Washington, D.C., November 1999.

[3]Recently, *2001 Kids Count Data Book*, Annie E. Casey Foundation.

[4]Recently, Mortenson, Thomas G., *High School Graduation Trends and Patterns 1981 to 2000*, Postsecondary Education Opportunity, June 2001.

Measure/source	Description
Status Dropout Rates	**Measure the portion of individuals within a particular age group (typically young adults) who are not enrolled in a high school program and have not completed high school**
National Status Rates (NCES & Annie E. Casey Foundation)	NCES uses data from the CPS to calculate the national status dropout rate, which it defines as the proportion of 16- to 24-year-olds who are not enrolled in a high school program and have not completed high school. The Annie E. Casey Foundation also uses CPS data to calculate a national status dropout rates, but for a smaller age-range – 16- to 19-year-olds. Both sources consider those who earn an alternative credential, such as a GED, to have completed high school.
State Status Rates (Annie E. Casey Foundation)	The Annie E. Casey Foundation also uses data from CPS to calculate status dropout rates for each state. However, because of the small sample sizes for some states the margins of error are large and there is no statistically significant difference in the dropout rate between many states with similar rates.
Cohort Dropout Rate	**Measures what portion of a group of students, usually in a single grade, drop out over a period of time**
Cohort Rate (NCES)	Based on data collected through its National Education Longitudinal Study of 1988 —which followed an 1988 eighth-grade student cohort through four waves of data collection (1988, 1990, 1992, and 1994)—NCES periodically reports a cohort dropout rate for various time intervals between 1988 and 1994.[a]
Completion Measures	**Represent the proportion of young adults, not enrolled in high school or below, who are defined as having completed high school. Depending on the measure, "completion" may be characterized by a single benchmark, such as receipt of a diploma, or, more frequently, includes high-school equivalence (e.g., GED) and, in some cases, nondegree certification (e.g., certificate of attendance).**
National and State High School Completion Rates (NCES)	Using data from the CPS, NCES computes completion rates, which it defines as the proportion of 18- to 24-year-olds, not currently enrolled in high school or below, who have a high school diploma or the equivalent. NCES typically also reports completion rates excluding alternative credentials, but did not do so in <u>Dropout Rates in the United States: 2000</u> and probably will not do so in its 2001 report because of changes being made to the CPS. State rates are based on a 3-year average of data while national rates are computed from both 3-year and 1-year databases.
National and State "Regular" High School Graduation Rates (Center for the Study of Opportunity in Higher Education)	This rate represents the number of students who, in a given year, complete a regular high school program and earn a diploma. This rate compares the number of diploma-earning graduates with the number of students enrolled in the ninth-grade 4 years earlier. The data for this measure are collected by NCES through the CCD collection from state education agencies.

[a]In addition, in its publications, NCES has compared these rates with those obtained a decade earlier through its related longitudinal study, High School & Beyond (HS&B).

Sources: NCES, *Dropout Rates in the United States: 2000, Dropout Rates in the United States: 1998*, and *Dropout Rates in the United States: 1995*, U.S. Department of Education, Office of Educational Research and Improvement; *High School Dropout Rates*, U.S. Department of Education, Office of Educational Research and Improvement, National Institute on the Education of At-Risk Students, Consumer Guide, Number 16, March 1996; Annie E. Casey Foundation, *2001 Kids Count Data Book*; and Mortenson, Thomas G., *High School Graduation Trends and Patterns 1981 to 2000*, Postsecondary Education Opportunity, June 2001.

Appendix III: Federal Programs That Can Be Used for Dropout Prevention

Table 4 lists 23 federal programs that federal, state, and local officials identified as programs from which funds are used to serve at-risk youth, which in turn could help to prevent their dropping out. Thus, these programs provide funds that can be used for dropout prevention activities.

Table 4: Federal Programs That Can Be Used for Dropout Prevention

Program	Federal Department
Junior Reserve Officer Training Corps (JROTC)	U.S. Department of Defense
21st Century Community Learning Centers	U.S. Department of Education
Carl D. Perkins Vocational and Technical Education Act of 1998	U.S. Department of Education
Comprehensive School Reform Demonstration Program	U.S. Department of Education
Developing Hispanic-Serving Institutions	U.S. Department of Education
Elementary and Secondary Education Act (ESEA) Title I, part A – Basic Grants	U.S. Department of Education
Gaining Early Awareness and Readiness for Undergraduate Programs	U.S. Department of Education
High School Reform State Grant Program	U.S. Department of Education
Indian Education Discretionary Grants	U.S. Department of Education
Indian Education Formula Grants	U.S. Department of Education
Migrant Education Program	U.S. Department of Education
Safe and Drug-Free Schools and Communities Governor's Program	U.S. Department of Education
Smaller Learning Communities Program	U.S. Department of Education
Upward Bound	U.S. Department of Education
Head Start Program	U.S. Department of Health and Human Services
Independent Living Program	U.S. Department of Health and Human Services
Temporary Assistance to Needy Families	U.S. Department of Health and Human Services
Office of Juvenile Justice and Delinquency Prevention (OJJDP) Formula Grants Program	U.S. Department of Justice
Title V Community Prevention Grants Program	U.S. Department of Justice
OJJDP's Truancy Reduction Demonstration Program	U.S. Department of Justice
Migrant Seasonal Farmworker Program	U.S. Department of Labor
Youth Activities	U.S. Department of Labor
Youth Opportunity Grants	U.S. Department of Labor

Appendix IV: High School Completion Rates, October 1998 Through 2000

State	Completion rate (percent)
Alabama	81.6
Alaska	93.3
Arizona	73.5
Arkansas	84.1
California	82.5
Colorado	81.6
Connecticut	91.7
Delaware	91.0
District of Columbia	88.0
Florida	84.6
Georgia	83.5
Hawaii	91.8
Idaho	86.4
Illinois	87.1
Indiana	89.4
Iowa	90.8
Kansas	90.4
Kentucky	86.2
Louisiana	82.1
Maine	94.5
Maryland	87.4
Massachusetts	90.9
Michigan	89.2
Minnesota	91.9
Mississippi	82.3
Missouri	92.6
Montana	91.1
Nebraska	91.3
Nevada	77.9
New Hampshire	85.1
New Jersey	90.1
New Mexico	83.0
New York	86.3
North Carolina	86.1
North Dakota	94.4
Ohio	87.7
Oklahoma	85.7
Oregon	82.3
Pennsylvania	89.0
Rhode Island	87.9
South Carolina	85.1

State	Completion rate (percent)
South Dakota	92.0
Tennessee	89.0
Texas	79.4
Utah	90.0
Vermont	90.8
Virginia	87.3
Washington	87.4
West Virginia	89.6
Wisconsin	90.0
Wyoming	86.5

Note: This appendix presents high school completion rates of 18- through 24-year-olds not currently enrolled in high school or below.

Source: Dropout Rates in the United States: 2000, U.S. Department of Education, National Center for Education Statistics, NCES 2002-114, Washington, D.C., November 2001, table B9, pp. 41-42.

Appendix V: Comments From the Department of Education

UNITED STATES DEPARTMENT OF EDUCATION

THE DEPUTY SECRETARY

January 14, 2002

Ms. Marnie S. Shaul
Director, Education, Workforce, and Income Security Issues
General Accounting Office
Washington, DC 20548

Dear Ms. Shaul:

Thank you for the opportunity to review and comment on the draft report, *School Dropouts: Education Could Play a Stronger Role in Identifying and Disseminating Promising Prevention Strategies*. The Secretary and I appreciate your helping to highlight both the extent of the national dropout problem and the need for further efforts to address it.

We concur with your assessment that dropping out is a serious issue for American schools. An overall dropout rate of close to 12 percent over the last decade is unacceptable, as are the even higher rates of dropout experienced in some regions of the country and among some groups of students. We view these statistics as a further call for the school improvement efforts proposed by the President in his *No Child Left Behind* education blueprint and adopted by Congress in the reauthorization of the Elementary and Secondary Education Act. In this letter we would like to provide additional information about relevant Department programs and activities, and to respond to your recommendations regarding research, evaluation, and dissemination activities.

New Efforts to Promote Student Success

The Department considers high school completion to be a key indicator of student and school success, and is actively taking steps to ensure that more students achieve this important milestone. These steps include two aimed directly at high schools:

- *High School Accountability*: Provisions in the recently passed *No Child Left Behind Act* emphasize improvement in high school graduation rates as a measure against which Title I schools will be held accountable.

- *New High School Initiative*: The Department is planning for a new "high school" initiative, designed to improve academic performance and preparation for college and careers; raising graduation rates will be one objective of this effort.

The report also notes that dropping out of school is a result of a long process of disengagement from school. The *No Child Left Behind Act* is an important opportunity to reform schools and promote student success in the early grades, before the process of disengagement can begin or take hold.

400 MARYLAND AVE., S.W., WASHINGTON, D.C. 20202-0500
www.ed.gov

Our mission is to ensure equal access to education and to promote educational excellence throughout the Nation.

Page 2 – Ms. Marnie S. Shaul

Research has shown, for example, that poor academic performance is the best predictor of who will drop out of school. Students who receive low grades, perform poorly on tests, are retained in grade, or are absent frequently are more likely to drop out before completing high school than are their peers. *No Child Left Behind* will apply proven strategies -- high state standards, annual testing of students in grades three through eight in reading and mathematics, increased accountability for student performance, reduced bureaucracy and greater flexibility for states, school districts, and schools, and expanded options for parents to make choices for their children's education -- to strengthen federal support for state and local efforts to improve student achievement. Annual testing of students in reading and mathematics should provide teachers with current information on a child's progress in school and enable teachers to arrange for the types of support and remediation that are most likely to help that child succeed academically.

The Need for Additional Research, Evaluation and Dissemination on Dropout Prevention

The Department supports a variety of information-gathering activities about dropout prevention programs and strategies. Currently, several national research and development centers funded by the Department's Office of Educational Research and Improvement are working on topics related to improving student retention and achievement; these include the Center for Research on the Education of Students Placed at Risk, the Laboratory for Success, and the Center for Research on Education, Diversity, and Excellence. As indicated in the report, the Department also funds evaluations of federal dropout prevention programs. An important addition to that discussion would be the use of experimental methods, the most rigorous approach to analyzing program effectiveness, in several of those evaluations. The discussion should also underscore the difficulty presented by the use of numerous definitions of dropout rates. The report mentions the multiple definitions that are used to count dropouts, but does not discuss whether it is advantageous to create a uniform definition that states would be required to report on as a condition of receiving financial assistance.

We agree that additional rigorous evidence is needed. In response to your recommendation to review the quality of existing research, the Department will consider commissioning a systematic review of the literature on this topic, of the kind and quality prepared by the National Institute of Child Health and Human Development on early reading strategies.

Page 3 – Ms. Marnie S. Shaul

It is the Department's intention that all of these activities maintain the highest standards of evidence. In particular, new studies of federally funded programs and other state and local dropout and reentry programs will emphasize the use of experimental designs and other rigorous methods.

Thank you again for the opportunity to address the important issues the report raises.

Sincerely,

William D. Hansen

Appendix VI: GAO Contacts and Acknowledgments

GAO Contacts

Diana M. Pietrowiak, (202) 512-6239
Charles M. Novak, (206) 287-4794

Acknowledgments

In addition to those named above, Susan Chin, Amy Gleason Carroll, Jeffrey Rueckhaus, Charles Shervey, and Anjali Tekchandani made key contributions to this report.

Bibliography

Alexander, Karl, Doris Entwisle and Nader Kabbani, *The Dropout Process in Life Course Perspective: Part I, Profiling Risk Factors at Home and School*, Johns Hopkins University, Baltimore, Maryland, 2000.

Cardenas, Jose A., Maria Robledo Montecel, Josie D. Supik, and Richard J. Harris, *The Coca-Cola Valued Youth Program: Dropout Prevention Strategies for At-Risk Students*, Texas Researcher, Volume 3, Winter 1992.

Cotton, Kathleen, *School Size, School Climate, and Student Performance*, School Improvement Research Series, Close-Up #20, Northwest Regional Educational Laboratory, 1997.

Dynarski, Mark, Philip Gleason, Anu Rangarajan, Robert, Wood, *Impacts of Dropout Prevention Programs*, *Final Report*, Mathematica Policy Research, Inc., Princeton, New Jersey, 1998.

_____, *Impacts of School Restructuring Initiatives*, *Final Report*, Mathematica Policy Research, Inc., Princeton, New Jersey, 1998.

Finn, Jeremy D., *Withdrawing From School*, Review of Educational Research, Summer 1989, Volume 59, Number 2.

Gleason, Philip, Mark Dynarski, *Do We Know Whom To Serve?*, Issues in Using Risk Factors to Identify Dropouts, Mathematica Policy Research, Inc., Princeton, New Jersey, June 1998.

Greene, Jay P., *High School Graduation Rates in the United States*, Center for Civic Innovation at the Manhattan Institute for Policy Research, November 2001.

Kemple, James J., *Career Academies: Impact on Students' Initial Transitions to Post-Secondary Education and Employment*, New York: Manpower Demonstration Research Corporation, December 2001.

Kemple, James J., Jason C. Snipes, *Career Academies: Impact on Students' Engagement and Performance in High School*, Manpower Demonstration Research Corporation, New York, 2000.

Kaufman, Philip, Denise Bradby, *Characteristics of At-Risk Students in NELS:88*, U.S. Department of Education, National Center for Education Statistics, NCES 92-042, Washington, D.C., 1992.

Kaufman, Phillip, Jin Y. Kwon, Steve Klein, Christopher D. Chapman, *Dropout Rates in the United States: 1998*, U.S. Department of Education, National Center for Education Statistics, NCES 2000-022,Washington, D.C., November 1999.

Kaufman, Phillip, Martha Naomi Alt, Christopher D. Chapman, *Dropout Rates in the United States: 2000*, U.S. Department of Education, National Center for Education Statistics, NCES 2002-114,Washington, D.C., November 2001.

McMillen, Marilyn, *Dropout Rates in the United States: 1995*, U.S. Department of Education, National Center for Education Statistics, NCES 97-473, Washington, D.C., July 1997.

Mortenson, Thomas G., *High School Graduation Trends and Patterns 1981 to 2000*, Postsecondary Education Opportunity, June 2001

Rossi, Robert J, *Evaluation of Projects Funded by the School Dropout Demonstration Assistance Program, Final Evaluation Report*, American Institutes for Research, Palo Alto, California, 1993.

Slavin, Robert E., Olatokumbo S. Fashola, *Show Me the Evidence! Proven and Promising Programs for America's Schools*, Corwin Press, Inc., 1998.

U.S. General Accounting Office, *At-Risk and Delinquent Youth: Multiple Federal Programs Raise Efficiency Questions* (GAO/HEHS-96-34, Mar. 6, 1996).

_____, *At-Risk Youth: School-Community Collaborations Focus on Improving Student Outcomes* (GAO-01-66, Oct. 10, 2000).

_____, *Hispanics' Schooling: Risk Factors for Dropping Out and Barriers to Resuming Education* (GAO/PEMD-94-24, July 27, 1994).

_____, *School Dropouts: Survey of Local Programs* (GAO/HRD-87-108, July 20, 1987).

Wirt, John, Thomas Snyder, Jennifer Sable, Susan P. Choy, Yupin Bae, Janis Stennett, Allison Gruner, Marianne Perie, *The Condition of Education 1998*, U.S. Department of Education, National Center for Education Statistics, NCES 98-013, Washington, D.C., October 1998.

GAO's Mission	The General Accounting Office, the investigative arm of Congress, exists to support Congress in meeting its constitutional responsibilities and to help improve the performance and accountability of the federal government for the American people. GAO examines the use of public funds; evaluates federal programs and policies; and provides analyses, recommendations, and other assistance to help Congress make informed oversight, policy, and funding decisions. GAO's commitment to good government is reflected in its core values of accountability, integrity, and reliability.
Obtaining Copies of GAO Reports and Testimony	The fastest and easiest way to obtain copies of GAO documents is through the Internet. GAO's Web site (www.gao.gov) contains abstracts and full-text files of current reports and testimony and an expanding archive of older products. The Web site features a search engine to help you locate documents using key words and phrases. You can print these documents in their entirety, including charts and other graphics. Each day, GAO issues a list of newly released reports, testimony, and correspondence. GAO posts this list, known as "Today's Reports," on its Web site daily. The list contains links to the full-text document files. To have GAO e-mail this list to you every afternoon, go to www.gao.gov and select "Subscribe to daily e-mail alert for newly released products" under the GAO Reports heading.

Order by Mail or Phone	The first copy of each printed report is free. Additional copies are $2 each. A check or money order should be made out to the Superintendent of Documents. GAO also accepts VISA and Mastercard. Orders for 100 or more copies mailed to a single address are discounted 25 percent. Orders should be sent to:
	
	U.S. General Accounting Office
	P.O. Box 37050
	Washington, D.C. 20013
	
	To order by Phone: Voice: (202) 512-6000
	                         TDD: (202) 512-2537
	                         Fax: (202) 512-6061

Visit GAO's Document Distribution Center	GAO Building Room 1100, 700 4th Street, NW (corner of 4th and G Streets, NW) Washington, D.C. 20013
To Report Fraud, Waste, and Abuse in Federal Programs	Contact: Web site: www.gao.gov/fraudnet/fraudnet.htm, E-mail: fraudnet@gao.gov, or 1-800-424-5454 or (202) 512-7470 (automated answering system).
Public Affairs	Jeff Nelligan, Managing Director, NelliganJ@gao.gov (202) 512-4800 U.S. General Accounting Office, 441 G. Street NW, Room 7149, Washington, D.C. 20548

 PRINTED ON RECYCLED PAPER

DATE DUE

CPSIA information can be obtained at www.ICGtesting.com

228317LV00004B/148/P